★★★ The

2012 BIBLICAL GUIDE TO VOTING

★ ★ ★ ★ ★

★★★ *The* ★★★

2012
BIBLICAL
GUIDE TO
VOTING

★ ★ ★ ★ ★

Most CHARISMA HOUSE BOOK GROUP products are available at special quantity discounts for bulk purchase for sales promotions, premiums, fund-raising, and educational needs. For details, write Charisma House Book Group, 600 Rinehart Road, Lake Mary, Florida 32746, or telephone (407) 333-0600.

THE 2012 BIBLICAL GUIDE TO VOTING
Published by FrontLine
Charisma Media/Charisma House Book Group
600 Rinehart Road
Lake Mary, Florida 32746
www.charismahouse.com

Cover design by Justin Evans
Design Director: Bill Johnson

Library of Congress Cataloging-in-Publication Data

The 2012 biblical guide to voting : from the publisher of Frontline Books.
    p. cm.
  Includes bibliographical references and index.
  ISBN 978-1-61638-466-1 (trade paper) -- ISBN 978-1-61638-581-1 (e-book) 1. Christianity and politics--United States. 2. Presidents--United States--Election--2012.
3. Bible and politics. I. Frontline Books.
  BR526.M24 2011
  261.7--dc23

                                        2011017052

E-book ISBN: 978-1-61638-581-1

11 12 13 14 15 — 9 8 7 6 5 4 3 2 1
Printed in Canada

CONTENTS

PART III: NATIONAL ISSUES

AT STAKE IN 2012

W HERE DO WE go from here? And how do we get there?

Wisdom is the principal thing; therefore get wisdom. And in all your getting, get understanding.

—PROVERBS 4:7, NKJV

Never has our nation faced a time of upheaval and tension such as this. Since Election Day 2008 we have endured a near implosion of our financial foundation with widespread collateral damage in the form of a continuing recession; a subdued, chugging, and burping economic recovery; unemployment that remains painfully close to the 10 percent threshold; real estate values that have yet to find their bottom let alone begin to mount any form of substantial rebound; bailouts; layoffs; massive deficits as far as the eye can see; a lecture from the media elite that our civic discourse isn't civil enough, conveniently after their candidate was elected to the White House—recall how dissent was

1

the highest form of patriotism, but apparently only until January 19, 2009—and the cherry on the bad-news sundae in the form of a tin-eared administration that responds to the worst economic crisis since the Great Depression by ramming a multi-trillion-dollar socialized medicine new entitlement down the throats of the American people. It is hard now to decide what the larger insult added to injury was: the repugnant charade committed by Nancy Pelosi, Harry Reid, and the rest of the Democrat-majority Congress under the name "deem and pass," or the blatant hypocrisy across the county from the summer of 2009 and early 2010 as the talking heads of the media slandered the Tea Party with vulgar remarks night after night on television.

In hindsight, maybe we shouldn't be shocked by anything this administration has done since taking office. They stated with vivid clarity near the end of the campaign season their intent not to "let a serious crisis go to waste." And indeed they wasted no time concocting their "Stimulus Bill," a moniker so breathtakingly steeped in Orwellian double-speak you had to wonder if they themselves ever wonder, "Can we really get away with this?" They certainly did, and it's quite challenging to arrive at any conclusion other than the political Left of the United States viewed their stimulus plan as their chance to raid the public treasury with the same reckless abandon they utterly wrongly ascribed to their political foes on the right during the Bush years, and specifically during the War on Terror following the September 11 terror attacks. Make no mistake—the political Left in the United States shrieked for more than six years in all their Bush derangements syndrome glory against the fraud and opportunism they accused the Bush administration of in response to the 9/11 terror attacks—and then turned around and did the exact same thing in reaction to the financial crisis of late 2008 and the ensuing recession that defined the first few years of the Obama administration.

Within that time span there was also the Obama Apology Tour in which the president attempted to curry favor with every left-wing goon around the world by attempting to apologize for everything the Bush administration had done. One wonders how the free people in Iraq felt about that apology, while popular uprisings across the Middle East hear not the first whisper from Washington in support of their calls for democracy. They must all wonder how the priorities of the United States got so far out of whack so fast.

And now we look ahead at what's before us...

- What sort of economic fallout will there be in the years after huge deficits resulting from the economic stimulus?

- How will the freedom movements in the Middle East shake out in the long term?

- In the near term, will the instability of the Middle East and the corresponding spiking of oil prices completely derail the global economic recovery?

- How many candidates will join the fray for the Republican nomination? Will we be choosing between Newt and Sarah? Will Jeb Bush jump in?

- What kind of all-out blitz will the country be subjected to for the reelection of Obama, considering the raid on history the Left pulled just to get Obama in office the first time?

- Will the recovery have legs and start blooming jobs by the time the summer of 2012 rolls around?

- Or will there be some kind of double-dip, the recovery dragged down by the massive deficits and municipal debt at the state level or the slow-to-recover commercial real estate market?

- Will there finally be an energy policy grounded in innovation?

- And how much more spreading around of other people's wealth will we have to endure before our economy gets back on a solid footing of competitiveness and growth?

As believers, we know to take our cares and concerns with thanksgiving and petition our Lord in prayer. And as we said in the run-up to 2008, the first thing Christians must do is pray. Pray that the Lord will raise up godly candidates whose values are based on biblical principles and who will govern in a way that is in agreement with God's wisdom and honors the blessings God has given. And encourage others to pray as well.

Second, stay informed of where the candidates stand on the critical issues highlighted for you in this book.

Third, get involved. Speak up in support of candidates who hold biblically based positions on key issues.

Fourth, if you aren't registered to vote, register now, while there's still time to vote in the important elections this fall.

Fifth, contribute financially to the campaigns of candidates you support.

Finally, cast your vote accordingly. May the new president we elect in November of 2012 be a godly, wise servant of this wonderful nation who will lead us into a rich, wondrous future.

PART I

 ECONOMIC ISSUES

Chapter 1

PRO-GROWTH ECONOMIC POLICY

OUR FIRST BEST path forward from where the Obama years have left us is back to our entrepreneurial roots, specifically in the form of a national pro-growth strategy rich in economic policies that support and produce economic expansion and job growth. Not for nothing has it been quite truthfully said of our great nation that the business of America is business. We are a free people, the shining city on the hill that gives hope to the oppressed around the world. Our freedom is the air we breathe, and since the days of the Pilgrim fathers the truest expression of our own precious liberty is our heritage of free enterprise. A free people such as we enjoy the blessing of being able to freely choose how we organize and obtain the resources by which we operate our lives, instead of waiting for a centrally commanded authority to dole out a periodic ration capable only of delaying starvation.

> You are the light of the world. A city on a hill cannot be hidden.
>
> —Matthew 5:14

Chief among our opportunity-blessings is the choice to found, build, and operate one's own enterprise. In such an endeavor, each of us may compete in a free and reasonably regulated marketplace providing goods and services at value-driven prices to our fellow citizens. We are free to innovate, free to discover new solutions to old challenges from which we may become more competitive and serve our neighbors with ever-greater choice and value as we enjoy expanding prosperity for our families, our country, and ourselves.

In these tense times it bears mentioning that our blessings of freedom have a nemesis that has sought to subvert and destroy their bounty since Creation. It is the godless tendency toward the collective, which demands each free individual give up his or her sovereignty to a central elite and become a slave of the state. Collectivism by its many names down through history remains the common denominator in each failed experiment in social engineering. Every time this notion has oozed back to the surface for another try, it has resulted in the stunting and stifling of the dignity and freedom granted mankind by his Maker. It is important to remain vigilant against this scourge, especially in a season of such uncertainty when people everywhere may grasp errantly for any solution or hero promising to take away their problems and restore the hope.

Every valid candidate for 2012 will be known by

their proposals for governing visions grounded in stout pro-growth economic policies with competitiveness, innovation, and job growth as their key goals. Look for policy planks describing competition-friendly business tax proposals, making it possible to lower the tax burden on American businesses, which are among the highest in the world today. And recognize the candidates who grasp that Yankee ingenuity is one of our truest, most valuable natural resources and the one on which to base a new era of policies for growth and prosperity—because it is about the individual and his God-given talents, not depending on the government to solve every problem from the cradle the grave.

> Then you will know the truth, and the truth will set you free.
>
> —JOHN 8:32

Chapter 2

■ FISCAL POLICY

OUR NATIONAL DEBT exploded under the Obama presidency. Although it was primarily in response to the economic crisis, the spending has also included massive pork programs that have caused huge deficits likely to last for several more years—that is, unless the 2012 election brings fiscally responsible candidates to Washington as well as every statehouse in the country. First among the candidates' priorities must be a fresh commitment to balancing the budget, perhaps even including a new effort toward the balanced budget amendment that has been tried a time or two in the past couple of decades.

> Now it is required that those who have been given a trust must prove faithful.
> —1 CORINTHIANS 4:2

Just as the credit markets that froze up during the stock market crash in September and October of 2008 had to be "unwound" from their overextended positions, so also our federal budget deficits must be unwound from their massive splurges in spending these past few years, including the high-risk real estate holdings that dominated both Fannie Mae and Freddie Mac. There have even been calls on Capitol Hill for both Fannie and Freddie to be closed, which may be a powerful election issue to keep track of, and which candidate supports it.

> Since an overseer is entrusted with God's work, he must be blameless—not overbearing, not quick-tempered, not given to drunkenness, not violent, not pursuing dishonest gain.
>
> —Titus 1:7

The spending spree in Washington has gone on virtually uninterrupted since the fall of 2008, cranking our national debt to a level now equal with our gross domestic product (GDP). It is a recklessly unsustainable path that must be brought under control as early as possible. There will be few areas in the federal budget not considered for trimming, at least for a while, and that will include defense.

There is little gray area in this news. No person or entity, including a sovereign national government, can continue in perpetuity to follow fiscal and budgetary policy so blatantly guaranteed to boomerang on itself and cause massive destruction. All Americans, and especially God's people, must make their voices heard that our house must be and absolutely will be put back in order, and sooner rather than never.

Chapter 3

■ EDUCATION

OR YEARS NOW we have heard how the Chinese, the Indians, the Japanese, the Scandinavians, and pretty much everyone else across first-world nations have better performing school children than the United States. The data bounce back and forth between low scores in math and the sciences, to the more fundamental subjects such as geography and literature. It certainly makes for a great sound byte on a Sunday evening's installment of *60 Minutes* to announce that some random American student could not locate Australia or Greece on a map. Aside from the primary problems faced by our nation's schools—namely the outsized influence of the unions and their budget-busting costs each year—the decline of our education system is a competitive threat to our national well-being. If our students are not fully and robustly equipped through their schooling years to compete in the global marketplace, our country's economic prospects will begin to erode. As much as education quality and standards are matters affecting scientific discovery or medical research, for two examples, the strength of our education system is a much broader influence on our national vitality and future prosperity.

> You shall teach them diligently to your children, and shall talk of them when you sit in your house, when you walk by the way, when you lie down, and when you rise up.
> —Deuteronomy 6:7, nkjv

Education is the foundation on which free societies are built. The informed electorate is what our Founding Fathers envisioned for representative democracy. At the heart of that equation is a sound and thriving education system.

> Get wisdom! Get understanding! Do not forget, nor turn away from the words of my mouth.
> —Proverbs 4:5, nkjv

Candidates knowledgeable in the lessons of God's Word will present their constituents an understanding of the importance of building our schools at every level. Look for candidates who know that strong, excellent schools are the rich, fertile seeds from which are born generations of bumper-crop harvests in economic prosperity and national financial health.

> Poor is he who works with a negligent hand, but the hand of the diligent makes rich.
> —Proverbs 10:4, nas

Chapter 4

SOCIAL SECURITY AND ENTITLEMENTS

OUR GOVERNMENT ENTITLEMENTS, including Social Security, Medicare, and Medicaid, have been the eight-hundred-pound gorilla of the federal budget for quite a long time. In 2012 as in 2008 and virtually every election season for the past forty years, the issue of entitlements will be in play as a key arguing topic. But this time the conversation of necessity will be different.

For the good of our nation, the debate had better be uniquely different for the simple reason that the entitlements state of the United States is on the verge of threatening our very existence. Between soaring costs for medical care, the impending retirement years of the Baby Boom generation, and the massive new spending undertaken by the Obama administration in response to the financial markets crisis and ensuing recession as its ill-timed creation of the new health care entitlement, our federal budget is stretched so thin that dire consequences now appear more rather than less likely. Already the global debate about moving away from the US dollar as the standard reserve currency has picked up pace, with suggestions for replacement options ranging from the Chinese yuan, to the euro, to the so-called basket of currencies in which commodities such as oil might be denominated. Each of these alternatives would mean reduced economic flexibility and growth potential for our economy.

For the upcoming election season, listen closely for the candidates who demonstrate an understanding that Social Security and the rest of our entitlements are due for an overhaul and then back up their ideas about entitlement reform with policy prescriptions grounded in godly wisdom—caring for the poor and sick, and doing so with wise stewardship and consideration of the resources available. It is far, far past time our elected leaders in Washington governed from a biblically grounded reality instead of a generation after generation of grand schemes born of "Wouldn't it be great if…" ideas. We don't have anymore time to wait.

Chapter 5

TAXES

OUR TAX SYSTEM is badly in need of an overhaul. For example, each year Americans spend several billion hours and hundreds of billions of dollars preparing their tax returns leading up to Tax Day on April 15. If our tax code was not so convoluted and complex, our annual returns could be prepared much more efficiently, which in turn would free up several billion work hours of our time each year for more productive and hopefully useful and profitable purposes. Whether the Flat Tax, a value-added tax (VAT), or some combination of simplified and streamlined tax structures is the answer, the theme remains the same in each prospective solution—the very mechanism of our nation's tax system is bloated and inefficient, and its renewal and overhaul promise to contribute to our economy's renewed competitiveness and vitality.

> And he said to them, "Collect no more than you are authorized to do."
>
> —LUKE 3:13, ESV

Key among ideas to overhaul and improve our tax system is the question whether our taxes are too high or too low. Depending on the scenario in question, it can be very difficult to think taxes are too low when reading a report about government waste and abuse of government programs leading to corruption, or members of Congress flying to and from Washington DC in publicly funded private jets. But at the same time, it is challenging to think of our taxes being unnecessarily high when considering how important most of government's core responsibilities are, the things that our varying levels of government can actually do well, such as our justice system, national defense, or our local fire and police departments.

It is time to bring some basic common sense back to our tax system.

> Let every person be subject to the governing authorities. For there is no authority except from God, and those that exist have been instituted by God. Therefore whoever resists the authorities resists what God has appointed, and those who resist will incur judgment. For rulers are not a terror to good conduct, but to bad. Would you have no fear of the one who is in authority? Then do what is good, and you will receive his approval, for he is God's servant for your good. But if you do wrong, be afraid, for he does not bear the sword in vain. For he is the servant of God, an avenger who carries out God's wrath on the wrongdoer.

Therefore one must be in subjection, not only to avoid God's wrath but also for the sake of conscience.

—ROMANS 13:1–5, ESV

Chapter 6

HEALTH CARE AND INSURANCE REFORM

L IKE SO MANY aspects of our national life, staying healthy and treating the occasional boo-boo has gone from a simple neighborly transaction grounded in common sense—probably conducted by a handshake—to a monstrous thing that threatens to annihilate the household finances of any person misfortunate enough to need significant care of any kind. And however much the plague of malpractice litigation has caused costs to skyrocket, the underlying fact remains that our health care system needs to change.

> Beloved, I pray that all may go well with you and that you may be in good health, as it goes well with your soul.
>
> —3 JOHN 2, ESV

We in this country enjoy medical care that is the best in the world. There is not much valid debate on that point, but it is the access to that care that appears to work less and less well each year. President Obama's health care reform effort was misguided on most counts, but the one thing for which he could deserve credit was in attempting to improve the health care insurance experience that most Americans and their employers wrestle with each year in the form of ever-increasing costs that limit the financial flexibility of both individuals and businesses. To be sure, the president's state-centric solutions will produce more layers of government bureaucracy and waste, so hopefully the candidates we choose in 2012 will be able to take some of the general ideas of the Obama health care and health insurance reform effort and add some more realistic, commonsense, or market-based solutions to actually improve the weak areas of our system.

Any plan to rework health care and insurance must include these market-driven plans that can place value and choice back in the hands of everyday consumers, without forcing on them the massive costs of risk built into the system in its current form. An effort toward tort reform would go a long way to disincentivizing the so-called "lawsuit lottery" that as much as any industry has contributed to the massive inflation in health care costs to the average American.

Chapter 7

ENERGY POLICY

I T WILL BE important in 2012 to seek and support candidates who offer something extra in the area of our nation's energy needs—the added extra oomph and fortitude to actually push forward with energy policy ideas to the point of realization. We have lots of choices available to us as a nation for meeting our energy appetite, but for decades now the key missing ingredient has been the ability to take reasonable policy proposals and actually cause real progress to happen.

In the seventies there were programs by both the Ford and Carter administrations to turn our thermostats up and our light switches off, while through the eighties and nineties we either did very little while the price of oil was low or we continued on-again, off-again dalliances with electric cars for the mass market and broad-based but poorly considered mass transit schemes including rail lines and especially high-speed rail, which has recently made yet another reappearance on the policy and political scene in Florida and California. But in each case, the taxpaying public has only lost in each deal, and usually to the tune of billions of dollars in pork barrel programs that did little to change how our energy needs are met. Nor has there been any effort to sever our supply lines from hostile areas of the world that should not have any influence over such a strategic national economic aspect as our energy supplies.

> Then the kingdom of heaven will be like ten virgins who took their lamps and went to meet the bridegroom. Five of them were foolish, and five were wise. For when the foolish took their lamps, they took no oil with them, but the wise took flasks of oil with their lamps.
> —MATTHEW 25:1–4, ESV

To add to the frustrations, our oil production capacity has only *decreased* in the past twenty years instead of growing to meet the needs of our steadily growing population's economic needs. And the insult to injury is that due to overzealous regulation during both the Clinton and Obama administrations, there are fewer and fewer places that new or continuing oil drilling sites can be started. It is against this backdrop that support for the "drill here, drill now" position has gained so much traction in the past few years, especially during the gasoline price spikes during the summers of 2008 and 2011.

Our energy policy needs some backbone so that we can take advantage of the resources our Lord has blessed us with, from the oil fields off the coasts of Florida and California, to newer technological discoveries such as simple, homegrown biodiesel that could effectively place a refining capacity in any community. But to get to those new and better mousetraps, our candidates in 2012 must offer the will to push for those new solutions all the way to their effective implementation.

Chapter 8

ILLEGAL IMMIGRATION

A S A NATION of laws and law and order, our long-running crisis with illegal immigration presents us a uniquely challenging problem whose solution remains as elusive today as at any time in the past several presidential administrations, all of which have tried to tackle the issue and were unsuccessful. On the one hand, it is a question of enforcing fundamental lows providing for our nation's sovereign territory and thereby maintaining the integrity of our national borders. As a nation of laws, this aspect ought to be very simple to conceive of and fulfill—but we are also a nation of immigrants. We were, are, and, Lord willing, always will be the land of opportunity, a core ideal about our nation as dear to us today as it has ever been. We still believe that the opportunities available to anyone willing to work for them are proof of the freedom and liberty we cherish. The tired, poor, and huddled masses are as welcome today as at any time since the Statue of Liberty first raised her torch over New York Harbor in 1886.

> You shall treat the stranger who sojourns with you as the native among you, and you shall love him as yourself, for you were strangers in the land of Egypt: I am the LORD your God.
>
> —LEVITICUS 19:34, ESV

It is due specifically to the sacredness of this notion we hold dear that the immigrations system needs to be refocused so that every person desiring to immigrate to the United States has the chance to do so through a reasonably vigilant yet efficient system. No one should have to sit on a waiting list for ten years, as in some cases, just to obtain citizenship, while at the same time our physical safety need not be compromised and risk the danger of terrorist activity by unduly loosening the system, especially for politically expedient purposes in hopes of bolstering voter roles and perhaps tilting elections toward parties making larger promises of government support to newly arrived population groups.

Most importantly we have a holy charge to reach out to the alien and extend the hand of fellowship, and as a law-abiding people we owe it to those newcomers to welcome them by and through a system grounded in the laws that define the very nation they dream to call home.

Chapter 9

FINANCIAL REFORMS

THE PACKAGE OF financial reforms to be applied to the nation's banks, brokerages, credit ratings agencies, and various other financial entities is meant to shore up the system of safeguards and reasonable regulation that was missing in different degrees and that allowed the financial crisis of 2008 to unfold the way it did. In truth, the conditions that led to the market meltdown in September and October 2008 were set in place several years before then. But in the last few years before the bottom fell out, there was a distinct "foxes guarding the chicken coop" situation going on between Wall Street and Washington DC.

The new regulations will serve partly as a confidence-boosting exercise to both the rest of the United States and the global marketplace so that investors everywhere will know that their financial resources are under the supervision of reasonable laws that ensure legal and fair business rules are being followed and that the system is sound.

Candidates in 2012 will have to address this issue, but the serious candidates will understand that an over-response to the financial crisis in the form of too much regulation is exactly not what the American public wants or expects. *Reasonable regulation* needs to be the key phrase when considering the candidates and determining which ones understand and are willing to stand up for the critical role our investment infrastructure on Wall Street plays in supporting a competitive, pro-growth economic policy for our country.

PART II

SOCIAL ISSUES

Chapter 10

DEBT AND CONSUMPTION CULTURE

A T THE TIME of the credit crisis and market meltdown in the fall of 2008, the amount of household debt was several trillion dollars.* By the time the stimulus program, the Trouble Assets Relief Program (TARP), and the Fed's "quantitative easing" programs had gotten underway, the government had effectively offset the amount of household debt almost to the dollar. No matter what happened between Capitol Hill and Wall Street with Fannie Mae, Freddie Mac, mortgage-backed securities, or credit default swaps, there remained one shockingly clear common denominator staring us in the face—we buy too much junk that we usually cannot afford in the first place. Many Americans spent the middle part of the last decade treating their homes like a cross between an ATM machine and a slot machine. The easy credit in the global economy that resulted from the economic policy

---

* Mark Whitehouse, "Americans Pare Debt," *Wall Street Journal*, March 12, 2010, abstract, http://online.wsj.com/article/SB10001424052748703625304 575115672827553404.html (accessed April 18, 2011).

responses to the 9/11 terrorist attacks was like giving a new drug to an already addicted junkie. But it all fed into a broader condition felt not only in the streets of American cities and neighborhoods but also in communities all over the world. We have, today, through our technology a greater capacity to communicate and connect with other people than at any time in history, and yet we do more and more things alone and feel more alone every year. And at the end of the day we squander our blessings in desperate attempts to fill the void and the emptiness with more and more trinkets and toys to amuse ourselves, when the real source of purpose and fulfillment is God Himself.

> For it will be like a man going on a journey, who called his servants and entrusted to them his property. To one he gave five talents, to another two, to another one, to each according to his ability. Then he went away. He who had received the five talents went at once and traded with them, and he made five talents more. So also he who had the two talents made two talents more. But he who had received the one talent went and dug in the ground and hid his master's money.
>
> —Matthew 25:14–18, esv

It can be a very delicate thing to suggest the changing of behavior patterns across a wide spectrum of people, but as God-fearing believers, we have a call on our lives to live out godly standards of stewardship when it comes to our financial lives. In 2012 it will be important to support candidates who share a conviction for God-grounded policies that can shape and redirect the emphasis on consumption that has been so prevalent in our economy for so long.

Chapter 11

PRISON REFORM

THERE HAVE BEEN movements in recent years to improve conditions in our nation's prisons, but it is a situation that needs to be dealt with conclusively. There are men and women in our prisons who suffer severe abuse at the hands of other members of the incarcerated population, and in some cases the abuse is tacitly approved by prison guards who, in exchange for looking the other way, allow the abuse as a form of control of inmates that may otherwise cause problems. Overcrowding in our jails and prisons exacerbates the problem, but it also a problem that does not have an obvious or simple answer; indeed, we cannot just continue to build more and more prisons, while at the same time we cannot continue to allow convicts to become even more dangerous and violent during repeated and successive stints behind bars.

> Remember those who are in prison, as though in prison with them, and those who are mistreated, since you also are in the body.
> —HEBREWS 13:3, ESV

"For I was hungry and you gave me food, I was thirsty and you gave me drink, I was a stranger and you welcomed me, I was naked and you clothed me, I was sick and you visited me, I was in prison and you came to me." Then the righteous will answer him, saying, "Lord, when did we see you hungry and feed you, or thirsty and give you drink? And when did we see you a stranger and welcome you, or naked and clothe you? And when did we see you sick or in prison and visit you?"

—MATTHEW 25:35–39, ESV

For the LORD hears the needy and does not despise his own people who are prisoners.

—PSALM 69:33, ESV

To hear the groans of the prisoners, to set free those who were doomed to die…

—PSALM 102:20, ESV

This is not an issue that forces its way onto the daily front pages from year to year. For most American households, there are more pressing issues to confront, especially in a time of economic recession and recovery that remains fairly fragile. But as believers and followers of Christ, we have a duty to remember the prisoner and obey God's Word in ministering to them and helping them overcome the sin that likely caused them to end up in prison. And as we choose our candidates for 2012, it is important to investigate each person's position on prisons and prison conditions and what they propose to do about the prison system in general, but more specifically the treatment of those behind bars who are already serving their sentences and should not be subjected to additional, horrible abuse during their time of incarceration.

Chapter 12

SECOND AMENDMENT

WITH THE ARRIVAL of a liberal Democrat in the White House came a fresh round of proposals for more and greater gun control. While President Obama thus far has stated that he supports the gun laws presently in place, there remains tension between his administration and the gun lobby, specifically the National Rifle Association (NRA), about what, if any, new restrictions this president may call for, especially if he should begin to conclude that he possibly may not win reelection in 2012 and, similar to his health care reform effort, try to push through a handful of new regulations while the opportunity is available.

> If a man steals an ox or a sheep, and kills it or sells it, he shall repay five oxen for an ox, and four sheep for a sheep. If a thief is found breaking in and is struck so that he dies, there shall be no bloodguilt for him, but if the sun has risen on him, there shall be bloodguilt for

him. He shall surely pay. If he has nothing, then he shall be sold for his theft. If the stolen beast is found alive in his possession, whether it is an ox or a donkey or a sheep, he shall pay double. If a man causes a field or vineyard to be grazed over, or lets his beast loose and it feeds in another man's field, he shall make restitution from the best in his own field and in his own vineyard.

—Exodus 22:1–5, esv

Guns may seem prevalent to particular segments of our population, but there is a healthy tension between calls for heavy restrictions and outright bans on all personal weapons, and the rights guaranteed us in our Constitution's Second Amendment. No one would ever want to think of having to have to rely on the Second Amendment in any actual, literal situation against an overreaching government, but clear-eyed, adult understanding of the way our fallen world works demands that reasonable and free people always retain the right to own and bear arms. And while we pray the day never comes that our arms would ever be used for anything more than hunting or sport shooting and the simple pleasure of collecting rare and antique weapons, it is a fact that the freedom and liberty we enjoy from our Creator are in some small part maintained as a result of the private individual's right to own a weapon.

This is another issue that will not likely appear above the fold in your daily newspaper with any regularity, especially when considering the tensions in the Middle East and the still somewhat fragile global economic recovery; however, that does not minimize the importance of this issue and the seriousness with which candidates in 2012 will address this issue and include it in their platforms.

Chapter 13

GAY MARRIAGE AND "DON'T ASK, DON'T TELL"

I T MUST STRIKE many as something of an almost amusing misnomer to hear constantly about the gay population in the United States talking about the rights they fight for, or more accurately, simply demand while defying anyone to make so much as the tiniest peep in disagreement lest they be designated with the dreaded "insensitive" label. Aside from the legal right to marriage in all fifty states, the gay population is lacking very little in the way of material well-being or the denial thereof. For two generations at least, the gay agenda has repeatedly fashioned itself as the cause du jour and cause célèbre in direct conflict with what many among that group would consider to be the hostility coming from America's heartland.

While no one would reasonably discount episodes of violence against members of the gay community, it remains rather challenging, to say the least, to consider this community as an oppressed minority. Almost by the week there is a new television reality program, a new sitcom, a new movie, or a new political figure; recently even a few sports figures announced openly their homosexuality. The rest of the nation might reasonably wonder and want to ask, "How exactly is this apparently preferred and coddled identity group so horridly oppressed by virtue of their lack of the legal right to marriage?" Coupled with the tone of much of their public commentary—by and large, one long stream of insistent demands that would be more at home coming from a spoiled adolescent than the measured public discourse of a fairly powerful political identity group—it isn't really any wonder that the gay agenda, in hindsight at least, seemed to reach most of their goals relatively quickly and then plateaued to the background noise that it has been over the past several years.

It is revealing of the largely "live and let live" notion of much of the American public, in addition to knowing clearly the Bible's wisdom regarding this topic, that the gay community's demands are not taken as any sort of national crisis. So, in reality, maybe it is time for the gay agenda to close up shop, having achieved many of its ambitions over the past few decades. Once a political movement largely achieves its desires, there is the human-nature tendency to need to manufacture a steady stream of new challenges to confront and new villains to contend against in the court of public opinion. But even in the aftermath of President Obama's repeal of "Don't Ask, Don't Tell" (DADT), the gay agenda looks like a ripe candidate to, in effect, "term limit" itself out of existence. Our military servicemen and women will adapt to this latest round of social engineering forced on it, just as this issue was during the Clinton administration fifteen years ago, but it will be wise and prudent to select candidates in 2012 grounded in biblical wisdom who will argue against policy experiments such as DADT, especially in light of the reality that many of these demands by the gay community are barely needed to begin with for a political identity group that is by any standard barely oppressed or prejudiced against at all.

> Or do you not know that the unrighteous will not inherit the kingdom of God? Do not be deceived: neither the sexually immoral, nor idolaters, nor adulterers, nor men who practice homosexuality, nor thieves, nor the greedy, nor drunkards, nor revilers, nor swindlers will inherit the kingdom of God.
> —1 Corinthians 6:9–10, esv

Chapter 14

ABORTION: GODLESSNESS AS POLICY

THERE ARE FEW issues that are as divisive as the topic of abortion. The abortion debate continues to pit two fundamental positions against each other:

1. The God-centered belief that life is precious and that the beginning and end reside with God

2. The human-focused insistence that "rights" are created and conferred by mankind; therefore, the act of choice eternally trumps the nature of the choice itself

The abortion question remains a contest between pro-life advocates defending the unborn and pro-choice activists intent on seizing power over life that rightly belongs only to God. Abortion is an abomination before God. The circumstances in which a life is created do not alter the divine nature of its creation. Even when a pregnancy results from assault, nothing changes the fact that it is a new life and a gift from God. Every life has a purpose, intended by the Lord to serve His kingdom in love and gratitude. No effort by pro-abortion activists to invent shades of gray within this truth can bear fruit.

> For you formed my inward parts; you knitted me together in my mother's womb. I praise you, for I am fearfully and wonderfully made. Wonderful are your works; my soul knows it very well. My frame was not hidden from you, when I was being made in secret, intricately woven in the depths of the earth. Your eyes saw my unformed substance; in your book were written, every one of them, the days that were formed for me, when as yet there was none of them.
>
> —Psalm 139:13–16, esv

> Before I formed you in the womb I knew you, and before you were born I consecrated you; I appointed you a prophet to the nations.
>
> —Jeremiah 1:5, esv

> You shall not murder.
>
> —Exodus 20:13, esv

In 2012 the *Roe v. Wade* decision will have been the law of the land for thirty-nine years. Viable candidates for 2012 elections must begin to include policy ideas for healing the millions of women who have had abortions since the Supreme Court made them legal. In the nearly four decades since the high court's decision, there are thousands of our female population who, through abortions, have carried the emotional and spiritual hurts that result from aborting a pregnancy. Ministering healing after God's forgiveness would be a necessary and productive step in working toward moving our country away from the damage abortion has wrought.

Chapter 15

FAITH VS. RELIGION:
SOCIAL JUSTICE

How we help each other and work together was brought into new focus with the election of Barack Obama. The faith-based initiatives of the previous several years were moved aside in favor of the older model of sweeping government programs to provide services and benefits to the poor and needy.

There is generally a modest collision between two competing visions of social justice in which the needs of everyone, including the poor and the needy, are provided for. On the side of the more liberal interpretation, the role of government primarily is to provide for the general welfare of the citizenry, while a more strict view of the Constitution holds that there should be less rather than more government involvement in any given area of daily life. It has traditionally been in this equation that churches have provided a support mechanism where the poor or needy were served.

The role of faith in public life was pushed more to the

front of our national conversation during the Bush years. That conversation has largely continued since it is and has always been one of the key aspects of our national character. And that debate continues to span a broader difference between the meanings of a life of faith through a relationship with God in Christ and a more social practice of one of the mainline organized religions.

Salvation comes through grace by faith in Christ. It is also true that there are many in our country who are not convinced that they are in need of salvation so much as they consider a spiritual aspect to their lives to be sufficiently worthy of their time and membership in a local church. The Bible provides help in this area, specifying that works are not the route to salvation, but that faith grounded in the blood of the cross of Christ will thereby produce good works for the kingdom of God. (See James 2:26.)

In 2012 we ought to seek out candidates who ground their policy and governing ideas in the true and biblical doctrines about what it is to live faith as a relationship with the God who created the universe, through His Son, Jesus Christ. It is important to identify the candidates whose ideas for government programs place the dignity of the individual at the very front of the vision for the programs meant to serve them.

Chapter 16

RACISM IN POST-
PARTISAN AMERICA

O NE MINUTE WE'RE electing the first African American to the highest office in the land and we're excited and proud of ourselves and how far we have come since the civil rights movement first began to right the wrongs of racism. But then, the very next minute, we're back to tip-toeing on eggshells as a new version of the American classic *The Adventures of Huckleberry Finn* is published with the n-word carefully exorcised from the text in the interest of sensitivity and lessening the sting of the word, which appears in that novel a handful of times. So which is it? Is this post-racial America, where the dreams of Dr. Martin Luther King have come true? Are we finally measuring each other on the content of our character, or are we still judging each other by the color of our skin? The evidence in daily life might begin to indicate the former. People of color are Americans just like every other group; the only differences are matters of cultural uniqueness to be celebrated just as much as a German-American community may celebrate a neighborhood Oktoberfest or Italian-Americans hold a festival and parades each Columbus Day. Despite terribly sad examples to the contrary—certainly racism still exists as much as any other sin does—this appears to be one area in which our national life just may have made some progress toward living up to our highest ideals for ourselves, living under the knowledge that there is ultimately only one race, the human race, all created in the image of our loving God.

But for whatever degree of improvement there may have been in the past few years, it is a fact that racism is a most fundamental sin that will not magically disappear by the election of an African American to the presidency. While it is a healthy sign of our nation's progress in this area, it cannot be taken for granted without risking the integrity of the progress made since the civil rights movement more than fifty years ago. Perhaps the applications of policies such as affirmative action have achieved their purposes and merit only minimal use in the interest of vigilance.

Following the 2008 elections, we were told that we had entered a new "post-partisan" period in which the heated battles between Left and Right would be overcome by both sides engaging one another reasonably and fairly and without the constant demonization of one another. Now, heading into 2012, it seems as if that whole notion wasn't too terribly much more than an empty campaign promise that had a nice ring to it but apparently wasn't too realistically workable. The health care reform debates had barely begun when anyone who didn't want the whole two-thousand-plus pages of legislation ramrodded through

Congress was deemed hostile and insensitive to the needs of the poor and sickly, instead of what was actually true, which was that whole large groups of Americans simply wanted the process to occur with care and attention. Instead of not letting a good crisis go to waste, many Americans, especially the Taxed Enough Already (TEA party) groups, sprang up in organized opposition of the hastiness of the health care scheme. And this, in the supposedly new era of post-partisanship.

We have made great strides as a nation leaving our racial disharmony in our past, but there is plenty more to be done:

> For there is no partiality to God.
>
> —ROMANS 2:11

PART III

NATIONAL ISSUES

Chapter 17

CAMPAIGN FINANCE REFORM AND THE POLITICAL ENVIRONMENT

C AMPAIGN FINANCE REFORM enjoyed a stint on the front pages of daily newspapers recently when the Supreme Court decided in favor of the First Amendment and granted corporations and unions freer access to funding and participating in elections. Generally speaking it may have been a sound move in restoring perfectly reasonable First Amendment rights to corporations and unions, but it still makes one pause and ask whether this bit of campaign finance reform is necessarily going to be the sort of improvement people from both sides of the political aisle have been working toward for several years, at least since the original McCain–Feingold Bill of 2002.

On the one hand, there is no good reason a company or a union should not be able to support a candidate, especially since both entities already exploit endless loopholes to generate support for any candidate they wish. But in an era when it becomes harder and harder to track where the finances come from for any federal office, especially the presidency, it is easy to react to the Supreme Court's decision with at least a moment's concern whether or not this will turn out to help the system or merely make the financial games a little easier to spot during election season.

The campaign finance reform issue generally has revolved around free speech. Present-day campaigns are too reliant on money, particularly with the growing reliance on television advertising and a cloud of social media campaigns to position a candidate in the marketplace every bit as much as within the national conversation. Attempts to restrict the flow of money into political campaigns aim to make political campaigns less expensive. This argument has remained the central issue.

It is a well-known fact that of all the topics on which the Bible teaches, the subject of money is addressed nearly three thousand times. The cornerstone of the Bible's message on money tells us that, while money in and of itself is perfectly fine and that the love of money is the root of evil (1 Tim. 6:10), it is the use of money that more than any other example reveals our character and the condition of our hearts before the Lord (Ps. 37:21).

Chapter 18

TERRORISM AND THE AFGHAN WAR

B Y ELECTION DAY 2012, if we are blessed to have remained free from another 9/11-scale terrorist attack on the United States, it will have been just more than eleven years since that awful day in 2001. Even if terrorist cells might possibly have been occupied during the unrest and freedom movements that sprang up in 2011 across the Middle East, there will never again be a time when we can take our freedom and security for granted. We may have spent the first years of the Obama presidency busily arguing about stimulus programs and TARP programs and radical overhauls of the nation's health care industry, but that does not mean for one moment that the threat of terror attacks has diminished.

As President Bush described in the first months following September 11, the battle against terrorists and terrorism will be a long one, not fought and won in mass troop movements along clear battle lines, but over years or even decades of hunting down terrorist groups around the world to confront them on their own territory, and never again a few blocks from Wall Street. President Bush was right when he launched the surge against terror groups in Iraq, and it materially changed the balance of the conflict in the favor of United States and coalition forces. The surge eventually led to Iraq's ascension into a stable, mostly governable state in the global community.

Despite campaign rhetoric to the contrary, President Obama made the difficult and right choice to continue operations in and around Afghanistan. It didn't necessarily make the mission more winnable by announcing even a general notion of a time frame when US forces would withdraw from the theater, but in the broader perspective it was the right thing to do, to continue pursuing terrorist cells and groups along the traditional hot spots of terrorist activity in Afghanistan.

Iran and North Korea remain troubling players among the less stable nations around the world that not only do not denounce terrorism, but they also, to the contrary, claim terror against the West as a perfectly reasonable response to the injustices they claim at the hands of Western nations, especially the United States. The changeover in leadership in North Korea will cause years of guessing as to if or when the military and the new leader feel compelled to stir up conflict in an attempt to demonstrate their strength, if not danger. Up until now, North Korea has relied on periodic trouble-causing primarily to draw Western nations to the negotiating table to try and deal for more food subsidies as the North Korean people continue to starve.

Iran weathered its own freedom movement in 2009, but it is very likely the tensions beneath the surface will rise again, and Iran may yet face the same tensions that swept across Egypt, Tunisia, and Libya in early 2011. The Iranian people are educated and knowledgeable of Western trends and business practices and will not be held down by the ruling theocracy there for much longer.

Our president in 2012, whether a reelected Obama or a new president, will need to be as fully grounded as one can hope to be to handle the constant flow of unexpected twists and turns around the world as we remain ever-vigilant against new and potentially more destructive terror threats against the American homeland.

Chapter 19

ISRAEL AND THE MIDDLE EAST

I SRAEL IS THE cornerstone to global stability.

I will bless those who bless you.

—GENESIS 12:3

The land of Israel is sacred and will be through the end of days. When the State of Israel was officially established in 1948, the rest of the Middle East began working for her destruction. Israel has fought and won two wars, the Six-Day War in 1967 and the Yom Kippur War in 1973. In each she soundly defeated her opponents, yet they continue to regroup and threaten Israel.

Israel remains one of the United States' closest allies. Our nations are bound by solemn commitments to freedom and democracy. We share many common ancestral bonds, especially in the form of World War II expatriates who sought the relative safety of America's shores just as Hitler was beginning his extermination of the Jews throughout Europe. Now in the age of terrorism, Israel has stood with her American family in the pursuit of al Qaeda and the nations who harbor all jihadists.

The success of the American war effort in Iraq assured that history will look on this endeavor favorably. Contrary to the portrayal of the struggle between Western liberal democracy and Islamofascism as a mere clash of civilizations, our present confrontation is a battle between the forces of submission and slavery and the God-given notion of individual freedom through the sacrificial blood of Jesus Christ.

Second Corinthians 13:2 teaches that we must confront conflict and take the initiative to resolve it instead of laying back and hoping the conflict resolves itself: "I have previously said when present the second time, and though now absent I say in advance to those who have sinned in the past and to all the rest as well, that if I come again I will not spare anyone" (NAS). Had we chosen a pattern more aligned with the Obama doctrine of engagement and dialogue and attempted to neutralize terrorist groups through the United Nations and other pseudo-governing bodies, we surely would have encouraged even more terrorist groups to threaten not only our homeland and Israel, but also probably most other freedom-loving nations across Europe, Asia, and the rest of the world.

The United States has a sacred covenant with Israel, especially in the face of the ongoing threats from other Middle Eastern nations. President Mahmoud Ahmadinejad of Iran denied the Holocaust, questioned Israel's right to exist, and made repeated specific threats against Israel. His constant denials of a weapons program and hollow claims that Iranian nuclear programs are for peaceful domestic energy purposes have yet to be proven, while the ramifications otherwise remain deadly serious.

> "Now then, if you will indeed obey My voice and keep My covenant, then you shall be My own possession among all the peoples, for all the earth is Mine; and you shall be to Me a kingdom of priests and a holy nation." These are the words that you shall speak to the sons of Israel.
>
> —Exodus 19:5–6, nas

Psalm 122:6 leads Christians to pray for Israel: "Pray for the peace of Jerusalem." Throughout the United States, Christians are coming to the realization that the cause of Israel is, in fact, our cause. Believers in America share that common cause with the Jews in Israel in matters both political and spiritual. In 2012, remember that the candidates you choose must be the ones who recognize the duty that all Christians have to Israel in obedience to the call of God from the very beginning of His Word to pray for and bless Israel.

> For Zion's sake I will not keep silent, and for Jerusalem's sake I will not keep quiet, until her righteousness goes forth like brightness, and her salvation like a torch that is burning. The nations will see your righteousness, and all kings your glory; and you will be called by a new name which the mouth of the Lord will

designate. You will also be a crown of beauty in the hand of the Lord, and a royal diadem in the hand of your God. It will no longer be said to you, "Forsaken," nor to your land will it any longer be said, "Desolate"; but you will be called, "My delight is in her."

—Isaiah 62:1–4, nas

Chapter 20

■ FOREIGN RELATIONS

RESIDENT OBAMA BEGAN his presidential administration with a world tour visiting allies and not-so-friendly acquaintances on a respectable and earnest yet somewhat misguided notion that he needed to engage those other nations and make it clear that the one-sided problem solving of the Bush presidency was now finished and the United States of the Obama years would be more reflective and ready to listen to other nations. We supposedly were going to be more accessible and cooperative, making a much more conspicuous effort to live up to the highest ideals of our nation in the eyes of the global community.

Or at least that was the idea.

Although the wider world gave the new president plenty of leeway to present his case for a while, back here at home we were suddenly treated to a seemingly endless parade of apologies at virtually every visit the president made. It didn't help that no sooner had he taken office, he was in Stockholm to collect his Nobel Peace Prize for doing precisely what even he seemed not entirely sure. Maybe the first few apology visits could have accomplished the desired rhetorical effect. But it quickly became apparent with the first bow to a foreign leader that the president was seeking to acknowledge not that the United States in recent years had been somewhat single-minded in its pursuit of the War on Terror, but that the United States was just generally wrong for ever attempting to defend our people and our way of life, especially when having done so without first engaging the representative groups in any way connected back to the origins of the terror groups responsible for the 9/11 terror attacks in the United States. And, of course, we didn't wait for any permission-like consensus from the likes of the United Nations either. It didn't seem to occur to the diplomatic community around the world that the American public fully supported President Bush in his initial reactions to the 9/11 terror attacks, including military actions against known terror groups and their hideouts in the mountains of Afghanistan in the fall of 2001.

Now, heading into the 2012 election season, our allies and the rest of the global community have seen both sides of the American political spectrum, and if the rest of the world didn't already grasp where each side was coming from, they certainly have a better idea now. Both France and England elected conservative leadership, however relative that term actually is in practice since both nations continue to struggle under the sagging weight of massive, decades-long social welfare states that are no longer financially feasible. In truth, those two nations are a few years ahead of where we might end up if the current administration and congressional leaders of the same party continue on their stated path to remake the United States in the form of a social democracy similar to what Europe has had in many of its nations since World War II. But most of those experiments in socialism have begun to fail simply because there are not enough younger people paying into the tax system to support the expensive programs provided by their respective governments.

The president elected (or reelected) in 2012 will take up where Obama has left off, continuing to work toward global economic growth as the world economy recovers from the 2008–2009 recession, while attempting to manage through a time of unprecedented change and upheaval from political revolutions and freedom movements—which is good news in the grand scheme, even if they present some growing pains in the meantime—and what seems like a steady stream of natural disasters on a mass scale. Our hope in this country is for a leader grounded in the Word of God who will govern with humility and respect for other nations while making sure to look out for the best interests of the United States.

Chapter 21

AMERICAN EXCEPTIONALISM

WHAT MAKES US different? If we are exceptional, why? What is it?

Certainly our respect for the rule of law gives us a more level playing field than most industrialized nations have had over the past century. Freed from rigid social strata, we are free to move and improve our lives as much as our ambition and ability may provide, and all within the reasonable limits of our laws.

But there is something more, something deeper and broader that makes the United States different. No matter how loud the arguments may get between God-fearing, churchgoing Christians and nonbelieving groups, our national character is largely derived from Judeo-Christian doctrine that cherishes the individual life more than the interest of the collective whole. Our national motto captures it perfectly: "Out of many, one." *E pluribus unum* does not leave much doubt that it is the dignity of the individual that is the building block of our nation, united from many different families, neighborhoods, cities, and states to form one cohesive union. Our ally nations may get a giggle at us every now and then, the way we freeze, glued to our television sets to follow the progress of rescuers retrieving a small child fallen into a well. But it is episodes like those that reveal what we believe with our actions much more so than the words we choose to describe ourselves and what we believe.

Are we exceptional? Yes, we are. We always have been. We remain one of the last places on earth where objective truth has a fair shot at ruling the day through our justice system, however imperfect it may seem from time to time. Because we aren't perfect. We are fallen and living in a fallen world corrupted by every sin that human nature can throw at us. But we are free to help each other of our own volition, to lend a helping hand and an easy smile to tell each other, "We'll get through this, just as we have before." We respect each other and each other's property, but far more than that, we also respect each other's right to freedom and to have a bit of elbow room when we don't feel like being fenced in.

We are a nation grounded in godly truths, especially the one key truth as described in the John 8:32: "You shall know the truth, and the truth shall make you free."

Conclusion

CLOSING ARGUMENTS

I T IS TIME we allow for a little bit of earlier, tried-and-true wisdom without necessarily risking losing the gains of our progress in the past few decades. Maybe we allow for a bit of hill-country wisdom expressed in bluegrass music for generations, recalling times when life was a bit simpler, and maybe it could be and ought to be again. Maybe we should listen to some of the more observant members of Generation Y who discover they now wish they had been born in 1950 instead of 1980. Maybe we can listen to the wisdom of no less a Christian soul than Edith Bunker from the 1970s' television program *All in the Family*, when she once answered her daughter's question about how Edith was able to handle money so carefully and manage a household, saying, "I was lucky...I was brought up in a depression."

> Every person is to be in subjection to the governing authorities for there is no authority except from God, and those which exist are

established by God. Therefore whoever resists authority has opposed the ordinance of God; and they who have opposed will receive condemnation upon themselves. For rulers are not a cause of fear for good behavior, but for evil. Do you want to have no fear of authority? Do what is good and you will have praise from the same; for it is a minister of God to you for good. But if you do what is evil, be afraid; for it does not bear the sword for nothing; for it is a minister of God, an avenger who brings wrath on the one who practices evil. Therefore it is necessary to be in subjection, not only because of wrath, but also for conscience' sake.

—Romans 13:1–5, nas

Our 2012 elections will impact the world and the United States for many years. Our economic recovery needs to be nurtured and supported with pro-growth and pro-competitive polices. There is still a terrorist threat that will not go away by itself and must continue to be dealt with.

Christian voters remain the hope of this nation in the upcoming elections. We know hope in the person of Jesus Christ, and hopefully we are able to see past the static and noise of our 24/7 news cycle and partisan politics—hopefully, we are able to focus on the core issues. Followers of Christ are Christians first, Americans second, and conservative and liberal thereafter. Christian voters fortified with the truth of Christ are the voters possessing wisdom and discernment to cut through the smog from political strategists and talking heads.

May we honor our Father in heaven and carry out our duty as faithful believers as we press forward in this trying season of our nation's history. Take the truth and good news of Jesus Christ into the voting booth, and choose candidates who will honor God and bless our beloved country.

FREE NEWSLETTERS
TO HELP EMPOWER YOUR LIFE

Why subscribe today?

❑ **DELIVERED DIRECTLY TO YOU.** All you have to do is open your inbox and read.

❑ **EXCLUSIVE CONTENT.** We cover the news overlooked by the mainstream press.

❑ **STAY CURRENT.** Find the latest court rulings, revivals, and cultural trends.

❑ **UPDATE OTHERS.** Easy to forward to friends and family with the click of your mouse.

CHOOSE THE E-NEWSLETTER THAT INTERESTS YOU MOST:

- Christian news
- Daily devotionals
- Spiritual empowerment
- And much, much more

SIGN UP AT: **http://freenewsletters.charismamag.com**

8178